Barcelona

The Ultimate Barcelona Travel Guide By A Traveler For A Traveler

The Best Travel Tips; Where To Go, What To See And Much More

Table of Contents

Why Lost Travelers Guides?

First, we want to wish you an amazing time in Barcelona when you plan to visit. Also, we would like to thank you and congratulate you for downloading our travel guide, *"Barcelona; The Ultimate Barcelona Travel Guide By A Traveler For A Traveler"*.

Tired of long, boring, and biased guides out in the market that not only waste our time but also waste money? So were we! We continuously had to ask someone for the simplest things that could have easily been found if we could speak the language of the location, or information that should have been in the guide we were using at that time! As we continuously face this problem we decided we should create a guide that that would cover everything a traveler needs to know from the point of Arrival to Departure, and the Lost Travelers Guides were born.

When having our guides created we take a lot into consideration such as time, therefore our guides are short and to the point. But mainly we ask ourselves and other travelers what we enjoy during a travel and what we wish we had known prior to visiting the location and that is where the Lost Travelers guides excels. As the Lost Travelers Guide team, we only have one goal and that is to make sure that our guides are the best out, and provides the most value available.

Each one of our guides are created by a team of professional researchers and travelers whom account every detail about the location from a brief history to amazing travel tips including where to go, what to see and much more. Once our guides have been created we then go over and double check to make sure we are providing our travelers with a fun, engaging, informative and the most powerful travel guide on the market.

"The World Is A Book And Those Who Do Not Travel Only Read One Page"

- St. Augustine

Thanks again for choosing us, we hope you enjoy!

From the greatest football team to dangerous bull fighting, Barcelona has proven to be a city without limits. It is a city rich in culture and art and one cannot help but admire the beautiful buildings and wonderful people.

For you to be able to experience the real Barcelona, you will have to know where to go, what to see and simply indulge your whole self inside the whole experience. One thing is for sure; you will soak in all that this city has to offer and simply want to come back until you cannot help it but come back. So how did this great city come into being? We will start by discussing just that.

Chapter 1: Barcelona's History at a Glance

The history of the city of Barcelona starts in the second century BC. It starts as Barcino, a Roman village, which was the largest Roman village outside Rome. But the Romans didn't rule Barcino for long because in the fifth century, the Visigoths made this village the capital city of their empire then moors took over Catalonia.

In 801 came the Franks, under the rule of Charles the Great, who made Barcelona the capital city of Spain. This is when Barcelona became the defense headquarters for the Franks who were fighting the Moors who had conquered the rest of Spain. The reign of Jaume I led to Barcelona successfully expanding economically. It is during this period that other cities in Spain were taken back from the Moors.

There is a gigantic cathedral, the Sagrada Familia in Barcelona. Its construction began in 1347 and lasted over four hundred years.

In the period between 1808 and 1814, Napoleon's troops destroyed many parts of this great city. All this happened when the Spanish were fighting for independence.

The mid nineteenth century was an important time for Barcelona, as it became the most important city in the whole of Spain. In 1888, Barcelona hosted the world's first exhibition. This exhibition was held on the former citadel's floor.

In 2004, Barcelona became a bull fighting free zone thanks to a declaration by the city's administration. However, every Sunday, starting from 19.00, bullfighting was allowed to take place, in the bullring, without any consequences. However, the bullfighting window didn't last long since Catalonia, the only remaining bullring in Barcelona banned bullfighting. History has it that the last bull to die in the bullring died on 25th September 2011.

In 2010, Pope Benedict XVI inaugurated the Sagrada Familia after which the church building was raised to a basilica.

Well from the history above, you can conclude that history is being made every day in the city of Barcelona, so who knows what is to come tomorrow?

Chapter 2: Travel And Safety

Getting In

The main airport is Barcelona International Airport. The Airport has 2 terminals T1 and T2. The 2nd has subdivisions A, B and C but both are linked by a bus every five to seven minutes (it is a 12 minutes journey). Here are some things to look out for while at the airport:

- Tax-free shopping refund: it has an office, which closes at 22.00.

- Duty free shops: These ones open at 06:30 and close at 22:00. Keep in mind that these shops are very hard to find in the city so it is best to use them at the airport if you want to.

- Parking here costs about €1.35/hr, €9.45/day, €6.75/day from the 6th day.

- You can use luggage lockers located on the ground floor of Terminal 1, which costs about 4.60 per day for a locker, which is large enough to fit 2-3 large suitcases. Terminal 2 has no storage rooms. If you don't use the storage services at the airport, you can use those in the city center some of which include Locker Barcelona with prices starting at €3.50 per day for a medium sized locker, which can store 1 luggage bag. You can use a luggage collection service called no-luggage.com or Bags&Go. These will collect your bags from the airport then transport them to whichever location you want them to. The prices start at €10 for the first bag and €5 for each additional bag.

- While at the Airport, there is free WiFi provided by Kubi Wireless. It costs about €7.50 for 45 min, €9 for 1 hr, €15 for 24 hr.

Besides flying in, you can use other transport modes to get in:

By Rail:

You can use various trains from various destinations when coming to Barcelona. Some of the notable ones include:

- Rail

- High-speed rail

By sea:

Barcelona has one of the busiest ports in the Mediterranean featuring up to 9 passenger terminals, four terminals for ferries and seven terminals for cruise liners. You can get to Barcelona by boat from Algiers, Sardinia, Livorno, Rome, Genoa, Balearic Islands, and Tangier etc.

By car:

Keep in mind that the blue marked parking stations ought to be paid for on Monday-Saturday starting from 16:00 to 8:00am.

By bus (like Barcelona Nord, ☎ +34 902 260 606). You can contact for all bus connections i.e. both national (e.g. 18 buses per day from Madrid) and international.

Megabus:

This one offers coach services between London Victoria Coach Station and Barcelona Estacion del Norte through Toulouse and Paris.

From The Airport

The airport is just 12-14 Km from the city center. You can use:

A bus

Aerobus is the city's main shuttle bus service, which connects both airports with the city center Plaça de Catalunya. There is a bus leaving every 5-10 minutes (A1), and 10-20 minutes (A2) daily from 5.30 am to 1am. A1 line usually moves to or from terminal 1 while A2 usually moves to or from terminal 2. The journey usually takes about 30 minutes although this can take longer due to traffic jam. There are 4 stops along the journey i.e. Plaça de Catalunya, Plaça Universitat, Gran Via – Urgell and Plaça Espanya. Aerobus stops running at 1am but you can use the night bus service instead i.e. line N17 to T1 or Line N16 to T2 between 22.00 and 5.00am; there is a bus every 20 minutes. Riding from Plaça de Catalunya takes 40-50 minutes. To save the most on your travel, use bus 46, which serves T1 and T2. One way ticket usually costs about €2; you can buy it from the driver. You can purchase the Travelcard to save on cost especially if you want to travel to other destinations. The card is valid for about 75 minutes.

Train

This one is a pretty cheap and reliable option. Every 30 minutes, there is a RENFE R2 suburban train calling at Sants (the travel time is usually about 18minutes), El Clot-Aragó (30 min) and Passeig de Gràcia (24 min). The train usually terminates right next to T2 by section B and has a connecting bus service (green colored) to T1 (you need 15 more minutes to your travel time). The train has everything you need including facilities for disabled people. A ticket costs about €4.10 but you can use the Travelcard (T10) for about (€9.95 for up to 10 trips over any period. Each trip usually includes 2 bus, tramway, train and metro transfers within the 75minutes. The best places to buy the card/ticket are from vending machines at the airport or the tobacco shop right in front of Terminal 2B. You can buy a travelcard at Terminal 1 right in the tobacco shop just next to the arrival lounge.

Tip: Some of the low cost carriers here include Jet2.com, Monarch Airlines, Air Berlin, Norwegian, Wizz Air, Blue Air, Germanwings etc. If you are sensitive on price, you can fly to Zaragoza (using RyanAir carrier) then you can use a train to Barcelona (it takes about 1 hour 30 minutes) and this can save you about 35 Euros from London, Paris or Brussels.

Barcelona is a city with a well-developed public transport system. You can move around quickly till late in the night and the public transport system (FGC) is incorporated in such a way that tickets are valid no matter the means of transport used.

Taxis and airport transfer services

You can expect to spend €30-40 to the city centre. You can actually book a taxi or a minibus online.

Moving around

By Bus: *Tip*: When in Barcelona, smartphone apps are the best to use in order to navigate your way. They give you bus information in real time and destination routes via bus, train, tram or metro. The best is the TMB app.

The Barcelona Bus Turístic links to many of the Barcelona tourist sites that you might want to visit. It uses 3 routes (there will be a map when you board) i.e. the southbound line, northbound lines. Each ride takes about 1-2 hours. You can use the hop-on/hop-off format to get off risk free at any preferred stop then get back to another bus or any other stop. You can also stay on an entire bus then continue as you get off at different stations that interest you. The buses here are double decked and have an open-air upper deck to offer better views. There will be earphones in every seat, which play information about the different attractions. The tickets cost about €27 per day but if you want to buy for 2 consecutive days, you pay €38.

The Metro

This is usually marked <M> in many of the maps you will find. You will also find a detailed map of the city in every station. The costs are €2.15 for a one journey ticket but you can save cost on a multi-person 10 ride ticket for just €9.95 (2015) for Zone 1, which usually includes many of the tourist areas (referred to as T-10). You can also buy a 50-ride monthly ticket. You can use the tickets on buses, FGC (Catalan Railway

Network), trams and on RENFE etc. You can buy 2-5 day public transport tickets for unlimited travel on bus and metro networks (it costs about €14 for two days, €32 for five). Take care of the cards since the machine won't read bent or damaged cards. You can replace the cards at any of TMB's customer service centers. Operating hours are:

Sunday-Thursday 5:00 to 24:00, Friday 5:00 to 2:00 and Saturday 24 hours. There is a continuous service from Saturday from 5:00 to Sunday 24:00.

RENFE: These are not the same as metro so ensure not to confuse the two; the metro is underground/subway while the train is RENFE (Rodalies de Catalunya also known as Cercanias outside Catalonia). Note: Although the metro is ideally the best deal for tourists, other transport modes are actually integrated into ATM (this is a system, which usually allows you to use the metro, bus or train with a single payment and these include bus, Rodalies (Renfe), metro, [www.tram.cat/en/ TRAM], and FGC.

Here are some tickets that can save you some money:

The Barcelona ComboPass®: This non-official pass gives you 2-5 days of the benefits of Barcelona Card (described below) and hop-on/off bus Turistic and the Montjuic cable car but it won't really save you money.

The Barcelona Card: this one gives you free travel on public transport and up to about 100 free admissions to different attraction sites. You can buy the card for 2 or 5 days for €37.00 for a 2-day card and €62.00 for a 5-day card. You can book online in advance and save about 10%. But if you don't plan to see very many museums daily, it is better to use transport only tickets. Note: you cannot use the card on fun transportation options like funiculars (except to Montjuic) and cable cars.

There are taxis too and they are yellow and black and have a green light on the top. When the green light is on, then that taxi is free. A taxi is only flagged down on a street and nowhere else and it should not be fifty meters away from a taxi stand.

Tickets can be bought from metro stations and FGC stations at the vending machines or pay booths. In buses, there are only one-way tickets that are bought from the driver.

Bike

Barcelona has a bike sharing system known as Bicing with over 12,000 subscribers. However, due to the various demands/requirements of the different bicycle hire companies in Barcelona, the city's bike share system is not available for tourists. However, you can still use bike rental services, which is available for tourists.

Scooter: There are many scooter rental companies in Barcelona including Mattia46, Scooters, Barcelona Moto Rent, Rental Moto Barcelona and GoCar.

Exotic transport: You can use the old tram, known as Tramvia Blau that dates back to the 20th century. It costs about €4.50 for a two-way trip. You can also use the Telefèric de Montjuïc, which usually links to the top of Montjuic, with 3 stations. It costs about 10.30 for two-way trip. Another exotic travel option is the Funicular del Tibidabo, which connects Tibidabo with the viewpoint for about €9 for two-way trip.

Tuk tuk: This travel option provides various routes through the city and to the most visited tourist spots but the routes are dependent on your preferences. Contact them through info@ecotukbcn.com or call them on 93 5195700.

Segway: This option gives guided tours on the history of Barcelona.

Car: When you hire a car, keep in mind that parking charges around tourist destinations are often quite high at about €3/hour, €20-36/day. Also, keep in mind that the traffic jams can be hectic. This coupled with the narrow roads and a complicated transport system makes it better to use public transport as opposed to driving yourself even if you have a map. Some of the major companies that offer car rental services include Sixt rent a car [13], Hertz, EuropeCar, DotTransfers. You can look out for free parking spots for travelers around Moll de Sant Bertran, Guell Park and Font Màgica, in Plaça Espanya

Safety

While Barcelona is not a city of violent crime, it is known for something else and that is pickpocketing. In fact, it is the pickpocket capital of the world. There are many bag thieves and pickpockets in places with popular tourist attractions and especially Las Ramblas Street. They are also many in the metro stations and the Sants train station.

How To Avoid Barcelona Pickpockets

We are not saying that you cannot fall victim to them but we are saying there is something you can do to minimize those chances.

1. Dress in normal clothes

Simply put on a pair of jeans and a t-shirt not some khaki shorts and a flowery shirt (tourist uniform). Dress in a manner that does not attract attention to you. The rule is, if you can't wear it at home then don't wear it here.

2. Dress according to the season

Spain is not a place of tropical climate. Therefore don't put on the shorts. In Barcelona, they all dress according to weather. Kindly adhere to this dressing culture.

3. Keep the guidebooks and maps out of sight

Only get the guidebooks and the maps when you need to consult them then keep them away. They serve as the main clue to pickpockets that you are new in the area and thus an easy target for the day.

4. Watch your bag always

When you go to eat in a restaurant, don't put your bag on the back of your chair or on an empty seat next to you or even under the table. Simply put your bag on your lap and put your hand on it.

5. Do not display what you have

Pickpockets want to steal something good and if you do not store your items properly then, their eyes will be stuck on you like glue. Some of the things you should not display are:

- An expensive camera

- A camera bag

- A laptop

- iPad or iPhone

Never use a big bag or store your wallet in your back pocket. Do check if all the zips in your bag are well closed.

6. Don't put your phone on the table

Do not put anything on the table be it your phone, wallet or tablet. There are kids or beggars who will approach you pretending even to sell you a newspaper but as you are glued on them, they pick up what is on the table and before you know it, it is gone.

7. Wear your backpack in front

Do exactly that and ensure all zips are closed. For safety purposes, please leave your passport at the hotel. Avoid anything with thin straps.

8. Avoid physical contact

Beware of anybody or anything that touches you. Also, watch out when someone drops down something and asks for your help to pick it up. The other trick is when two pickpockets come, hug you, and act as friends even though you do not know them. Do not smile; push them away with all your might. These pick pockets never fight; they run when spotted. Do not hug strangers when drunk and do not accept help from anyone other than the police.

9. Be wary of street games

Stay away and do not dare to stand and watch street games because they are scams that are operated by criminal gangs. You will not only lose money while playing but since you are distracted you won't know when you are being pick pocketed.

10. Do not carry all your credit cards

Leave some at home if possible or back at the hotel where you are staying. If your wallet is stolen but the credit cards are returned, you should still cancel them because pick pockets do take photos of the cards and use them on online fraud.

11. Keep cash in another pocket

Have your wallet but let your cash be kept in a separate pocket. Do not put all your important things in one bag. Separate them.

12. Have a list of important numbers

This is to ensure that even if your phone is stolen, you can still recall important numbers or you can also call during emergencies.

13. Be careful at the beach

At the beach, there are thieves too especially at Barceloneta. Do not fall asleep here or leave your stuff behind as you go to take a swim. Look out for the person next to you because if they only have a towel and no book or lotion then watch out. Put your wallet inside the shoe and if you suspect anything talk to the drink vendors since they can help catch a thief and hand them over to the police.

14. Be safe in the metro

There are gangs that operate here so ensure that your bag has a secure clasp. Grip your bag and ensure your wallet is in the front or side pocket. One great tip is to put a rubber band round your wallet so that it creates resistance when being pulled out. You should also make use of your voice and shout when you suspect anything.

15. Do not drink too much

This is self-explanatory because the more you drink, the more vulnerable you become.

16. Report any theft incident to the police

Your money may be stolen but a good citizen will hand over your wallet to the police so do report.

17. Be aware of fake police

They are in plain clothes; they want to fine you on the street and they ask for tourist ID. These are fake policemen. The Spanish police do not ask for tourist ID nor ask for bribes. Ask for their ID first.

Information is power so the moment you know all this, you are able to ensure that you are safe and are free to enjoy your Barcelona trip.

Chapter 3: Barcelona's Sweet 16

Although there are many places you can visit in Barcelona, these 16 are a must-see during your visit.

1. The Sagrada Familia

Officially referred to as "The Basílica i Temple Expiatori de la Sagrada Família.

The Sagrada Familia is not only one of the well-known landmarks in Barcelona but is also the essence of art embellished in religion. It is a UNESCO World Heritage Site. The church is so huge that it is referred to as the cathedral yet it even doesn't have a bishop's seat. This building was inaugurated by Pope Benedict XVI on November 7, 2010 and is raised to a basilica.

Remember we said that Barcelona is a city in which history happens every day. The Sagrada Familia has been on the journey of construction from 1882 and it is expected to be completed in 2016! The main architect is Antoni Gaudi who worked on it from 1883 until his death in 1926. His influence on the building is quite significant.

You can spend an entire day in this church as it holds great biblical mysteries on its walls and facades. The church has twelve bell towers, which rise up to one hundred meters. For now, eight towers have been completed. The first architect who planned the church designed it in gothic style. He was Francisco del Villar but he only managed to start work on the crypt in 1882. He ran into disagreements and resigned after which Antoni Gaudí took over. Gaudí put his heart and soul into this project until his death. He called this church "cathedral" even though he knew it had no bishop's seat. He had a strong conviction that the city of Barcelona will one day be known because of the church he was working on.

This church is the most visited monument not only in Barcelona but the whole of Spain. This simply means that there are long queues to pay. The queues are devastating during mid-morning. As such, simply try to get there early so that you do not spend a lot of time in line. Do go during the off peak hours. Nonetheless, there is a good reason why people are thronging to see the church. It is the manifestation of magnificence.

2. Avinguda Diagonal

When you see streets, you simply see streets but in Barcelona, you don't see a street. You get to see the Avinguda Diagonal, the most iconic avenue in Barcelona. It is the longest and the widest and was designed by Ildefons Cerdà. This avenue is not just iconic for the sake of it. What do you think of an avenue that took a period of 126 years to be built? But it grew gradually. Its different stages and length make you stroll diagonally in a manner that you can clearly and vividly see its fine architectural features and get to learn about the history of the city while at it.

There are plenty of open spaces within this avenue. There is the Jaume Vicens Vives, Gardens are on the sea side precisely behind the la Caixa towers while on the mountain side there are two gardens between two streets namely C/ John M. Keynes and C/ González Tablas.

The avenue is also home to learning institutions namely The University of Barcelona and the University Polytechnic of Cataluna.

So what can you do while strolling diagonally? Well, you can do lots of shopping and sample some of the best cuisines in the restaurants in the area. There is no need to worry about transport because the avenue has nine metro stations and thirteen tram stations.

Metro stations on Avinguda Diagonal

- Zona Universitària

- Palau Reial

- Maria Cristina

- Diagonal

- Provença

- Verdaguer

- Glòries

- Selva de Mar

- El Maresme Fòrum

Tram stations in Avinguda Diagonal

- Zona Universitària

- Palau Reial

- Maria Cristina

- Numància

- Francesc Macià

- L'Illa

- Ca L'Aranyó

- Pere IV

- Glòries

- Fluvià

- El Maresme

- Fòrum

- Selva de Mar

3. Gothic Quarter (Barri Gòtic)

The Gothic Quarter was once a Roman village. That's why a visit to this place will show some remnants that show its great past. Today, it is all a fusion of the old and the new as new buildings stand side by side with old ones. This mix is what makes the place attractive.

Do ensure that you have your compass on standby or a Google map app because the streets here are winding and it will take awhile before you get used to the directions.

There are plenty of peaceful squares, which are referred to as placas. They are spaces where you can just take it easy and relax as you take in the beautiful surroundings. The main attraction here is the Cathedral, which is full of geese and plants.

After all, the site seeing and relaxing, you can sample the delicacies by visiting one of the many restaurants in the area. And if clubbing is your thing, the nightlife of Gothic Quarter will definitely be one you can remember.

The Gothic Quarter has a street known as the Calle Avinyo, which is filled with all the little boutiques where you can shop. If you are the type that simply worships designer labels then you can head on over to Placa Catalunya.

Tip: These quarters are the perfect place for an afternoon walk given that it is the cultural center of the city.

If you are looking for accommodation, here are some of the hotels around this area:

- Adagio Hotel
- Colon Hotel
- Gotico Hotel
- H10 Montcada Hotel
- Meridien Hotel
- Monte Carlo Hotel
- MontBlanc Hotel
- Neri Hotel
- Nouvel Hotel
- NH Barcelona Centro
- Rialto Hotel

- Rivoli Ramblas Hotel

- Royal Hotel

- Suizo Hotel

4. Park Güell

Park Güell is one of Gaudí's famous works. Located on the Carmel Hill (in the Gràcia district of Barcelona), this is a public park system, which is composed of gardens comprising of architectonic elements. The park was actually constructed between 1900 and 1914 but was opened in 1926. It was declared a UNESCO World Heritage Site under the "Works of Antoni Gaudi".

One unique feature that the park has is that it matches perfectly with nature and has wonderful split ceramics that are full of color.

The park can be accessed through several entrance points but the most grandeur is the Carrer d'Olot. This entrance has two pavilions, which have cafes on both sides. Go straight through the pavilions and up a staircase where you will see a dragon made of split ceramics.

Inside the park, there is the hall of columns (Roman inspired), which act as support for a large terrace inside. This hall was supposed to be a market. At the end of these columns is a very large ceramic balustrade containing a bench. It winds like snake lines and gives you a spectacular view over the city.

After the square, the entire green space is what is seen. It is thought that this area was a challenge for Gaudí since he had to make a work of art using nature and do so naturally. The result is astounding since it resulted into a maze integrated with bridges, walls, courses, and trails.

Eusebi Güell acquired the land on which the park sits on in 1885. He (Eusebi Güell) was an industrialist and Gaudí's patron. Güell instructed Gaudí to construct a garden city whereby nature and buildings would have a form of symbiotic relationship. Even after just two buildings, roads and the park, no one showed any interest.

Getting to Parc Güell

You will go to the station Lesseps using underground line L3 and then you can simply walk on foot to the park. This should take you about ten to fifteen minutes. Simply look out for a road with the longest name to master i.e. "Avinguda del Santuari de Sant Josep de la Muntanya". The road goes up to the main entrance. Here is a map.

All areas in the park are accessed free of charge but you will have to pay if you want to see the monumental zone. This is the zone where you will find the beautifully decorated dragon at the entrance, the market hall, and the curved bench. They only allow four hundred guests per half an hour.

You can purchase the tickets at the box office or simply book them online. The secret of the ticket is that it does not only get you to the monumental zone but you also get to stay as long as you like. Buying them at the box office means you should have enough free time to queue. As such, it is better to buy it online.

5. Casa Milà

Many people refer to Casa Milà as La Pedrera, which literally means "The Quarry". Located in Catalonia, this modernist building was designed by Antonio Gaudi between 1906 and 1910-it was actually his last building before he committed himself to working on the Sagrada Familia. This is one of the most impressive buildings in Barcelona.

At the front, the house appears to be a group of massive rocks, which have wavy iron lines and ornaments that are beaten .The entire building has two houses containing individual courtyards and connected by a façade.

Story has it that there was a couple who wanted to build a house on their plot to a certain noble and that this house was to stand out in the whole area. Mr. Pedro Milà, who was the husband, heard about Gaudí and his great works especially how given that he had just completed a house, Casa Batlló, for a rich man on the same street. He contracted Gaudí who started work on the house in 1906 and finished it after four years.

So why is it called the quarry house? Well it all has to do with its unusual mode of construction. Large stone slabs were mounted to the façade first and worked on by craftsmen. The house also has a ventilation system that is 100% natural: thus, there is no need for air conditioning. The original plans were that it has an elevator but that was built later.

The interior of this house is full of round shapes and natural colors on the walls. In the yard, there are stairs that twine and that go straight to the entrance of the house and most of the walls inside are mobile. Due to the strict use of natural forms in its construction, the house has no right angle.

The main attraction of the Casa Milà is found nowhere else but the roof. You do not only get an exceptional view of Barcelona but you also get to do so with soldiers who come in form of chimneys. The chimneys were designed in a manner that they look like soldiers watching over the roof.

Tip: Set at least two hours for your visit. This is one of the most visited tourist sites in Barcelona so you should expect some long queues at the tickets section. However, you can avoid the wait by buying your ticket online.

6. Casa Batlló

This house inspired the owners of Casa Milà to get Antoni Gaudí to build them a house like none other. From outside, this building looks like a tall tower of skulls and bones. You will see the skulls in the balconies and the bones as supporting pillars but all this is just the result of how Gaudí would stretch his imagination. He was also inspired by marine life as seen from the colors and decorations on the façade.

The best time to visit the Casa Batlló is at night because it is when the decorations come to life as the entire façade is illuminated. The visit will be worth your while, as you will learn how a great architect paid detailed attention to his designs.

There are audio guides that are availed at the front desk to give you information on each of the rooms in the house. These audio guides come in several languages including English,

Spanish, Catalan, French, German, Italian, Portuguese, Russian, Chinese, and Japanese.

7. Montjuïc Hill

This hill has witnessed and has been part of very important international events. The first of such events was the international exhibition in 1929 then the Olympic Games in 1992.

The Montjuïc hill is home to museums like the Museu Nacional d'Art de Catalunya-MNAC, the Fundació Miró, the Museu d'Arqueologia and the Museu Etnològic.

The hill holds the site of the 1992 Olympics, which contains a stadium, a sports palace, and a telecommunications tower designed by none other than Santiago Calatrava. Just next to the Olympic stadium, there are botanical gardens.

In the hill, there is the most spectacular and magical fountain called the Montjuïc Magic Fountain. The fountain, which was built in 1929, offers a colorful display of water acrobatics in fifty kinds of shades and hues. There is also music and lights. Every year, the magic fountain is the site for Piromusical, which is all about firework display, lasers, and music. The fountain operates on recycled water so do not worry that precious water is going to waste while it is a form of art.

7. The Palau de la Música Catalana

Located in La Ribera, which is an old section of Barcelona, this is the palace of Catalan music. This was built around 1905 for the choral society under the funding of the society although the rich and powerful also contributed. Just after its completion, the Barcelona City Council declared it the best building in Barcelona in 1909. Years later, in 1997, it was declared a UNESCO World Heritage Site.

The building has since undergone restoration and currently attracts more than half a million people from all over the world who attend musical performances in the palace annually.

Although it is on a cramped street, it really stands out bold in the midst of seemingly bold buildings.

The Palau is designed in a manner that is common of Catalan modernism where it is just curves and dynamic shapes instead of straight lines and static forms. The decoration is predominantly made of floral and organic motifs. Local craftsmen and artisans were given the freedom to create sculpture, ornamentation and other decorative structural elements, which have made the building famous.

8. Camp Nou

This is the second largest football stadium in the world and is home to FC Barcelona since 1957. It has a sitting capacity of 99,354 making it the biggest football stadium in the world in terms of capacity.

Work on the stadium started in 1954 and the construction took three years. It was built because of the previous stadium not having enough room for expansion.

Two UEFA championship games have been held in this stadium and it was used in the 1992 Olympic Games.

In order to get there, you can take the tram since there is a Trambaix, which is five hundred meters away from the stadium. Camp Nou can also be accessed via the metro and some of the nearby stations are Palau Reial, Maria Cristina and Collblanc just to mention a few. A bus is also suitable, as there are several bus stops close to the stadium.

9. Montserrat Spain

This is a Benedictine Monk Monastery far away on the mountains and it is just one hour away from Barcelona if you use the train. This is not just a place of religious essence but it is also a remarkable sight considering the natural beautiful surroundings associated with it.

If you are the kind of person who loves walking, then you will enjoy doing so through the mountain as you get a breathtaking view of the whole of Catalonia. The other thing about the Montserrat monastery is that it is famous for Basilica Choir boy performances of Gregorian chants along with other genres of religious choral music. You can hear them free of charge at 13:00 inside the Basilica.

The monk mountain also has a history to do with holy visions. In 880, a group of shepherd children witnessed a bright light falling from the sky and onto the mountain. At the same time, the children heard angels singing music that made their hearts fill with joy. The experience was overwhelming and the children ran back home to tell their parents. The parents went and witnessed the same and they concluded that the visions were God sending a sign. A local vicar also witnessed the happenings. These visions occurred in a cave inside the mountain and when religious researchers explored the cave, they found the image of the Virgin Mary and from that moment, the cave became a holy place for religious pilgrims.

The site where these visions took place is marked by a Holy Grotto and is visited by thousands of visitors.

10. La Monumental

This was the last arena for bullfighting in Barcelona. Its initial name was Plaza de El Sport when it was inaugurated in 1914. It was then expanded in 1916 (to a capacity of 19,582) with the current name. It is found at the confluence of Marina Street and Gran Via which are both in the Eixample. The whole monument is surrounded by a superior barrage. Ever since 28 July 2010, there has been a ban on bullfighting events.

11. Tibidabo

This is the highest mountain on the Collserola mountain range. It is approximately five hundred and twenty meters high and serves as a shield keeping the hinterland weather from the city. Visiting this mountain is worth it because of the clear breathtaking view it gives. On clear days, you can get a clear view of the Montserrat.

There is a legend that has to do with the name Tibiadabo. The legend relates to when the devil was tempting Jesus (in the Bible) to kneel down and worship him. The words are "Haec omnia tibi dabo si cadens adoraberis me", which in English translates to "All this I will give you if you kneel down".

You do not need to reach the top of the mountain before you get to enjoy what it has to offer. Take the subway line L7 to Avinguda del Tibidabo terminus then from here, get into the

Tramvia Blau. This has been the only tram in Barcelona for quite a long time and it is unique.

Before you reach the top of Tibidabo, there is the Parque d'Atraccions. This an amusement park with a Ferris wheel, roller coaster and a round about

Just a few meters from the amusement park is a church Sagrada Corazon that is similar to the Sacre Coeur, which is in Paris. The church, which is a Basilica, was completed in 1961. On the ground floor inside the church, there is church space that dates back to around 1900. At the top of the Basilica, a statue of Christ stands.

12. Poblenou Cemetery

Did you ever think that a cemetery could be a local art gallery? Well, I am sure that you never even thought about that but that is exactly what Poblenou Cemetery is. This cemetery ground is full of works of art and it has two important parts, the original cemetery, and the part that was extended in the nineteenth century.

The old cemetery was destroyed in 1775 by Napoleon's troops but it was then rebuilt in 1819 based on the designs by Antonio Ginesi. The style of the new cemetery has many elements that reveal that there was a heavy Egyptian influence in the designs.

The cemetery is the final resting place for eminent Catalans for instance the Malda family and the composer Joseph Anselm Clave. There is the tomb of the gypsies, which has almost alive sculptures for example a man with a packet of cigarettes in his pocket.

Prominent families in Barcelona have built mausoleums and pavilions that feature high quality artistry for instance the sculpture known as the kiss of death, which is traced back to 1930.

13. Museu National d'Art de Catalunya

This museum is inside the Palau National. The building is at the foot of theMontjuïc.

The Palau was at first Spanish Pavilion in 1929. Extensive renovation was done on it and it reopened in 1997. The museum shows more than two hundred and sixty thousand works of art making it the biggest and most important museum in the whole of Barcelona.

MNAC or the Catalan Museum Act was founded in 1990. It is the world's biggest collection of Roman Frescoes. There is also a department of Gothic statues and Frescoes.

14. Barcelona Aquarium

The Barcelona Aquarium is considered as not just a leisure center but also as an educational center specializing in Mediterranean marine life. It has thirty-five aquariums and eleven thousand animals of which are made up of four hundred and fifty different species. If you have never done deep sea diving or want to experience the National Geographic Channel one on one, then this is the place for you. You will get to see all sorts of marine creatures from sharks to sea horses.

One of the most attractive features of the Barcelona Aquarium is the Oceanarium. This is an eighty-meter long underwater tunnel in which you can walk in and feel like you are taking a deep swim in sea with all the other creatures in it.

The Sections of Barcelona Aquarium

The aquarium has three main sections:

1. The main aquarium houses majority of the underwater creatures for instance dogfish, octopuses and sea horses. Each tank has photos and descriptions for you to know more about the creatures. This is where the Oceanarium is found.

2. The Planeta Aqua area is for educational purposes where the importance of water is explained. You will also find penguins here. There are also all the lethal fish here.

3. Then finally, there is the Explora. This is mainly a place for children to let loose and play and this is great for families. You can slide down water tunnels or take photos of your children dressed in turtle suits. They also get to learn more about the under water world in an interactive manner.

In case you get hungry, don't worry because there is a cafeteria where you can grab some fries and burgers.

For those who are brave and are professional divers, then there is the opportunity to dive in with sharks inside the aquarium three times a week.

15. Zoo de Barcelona

The Barcelona zoo is home to seven thousand wild animals from four hundred diverse species. This zoo is something to behold. It sits on fourteen hectares in the Parc de la Ciutadella. The zoo was founded in 1892 and was inside the buildings that had hosted the 1888 world exhibition. Lluís Martí Codolar contributed the first animals in it.

The zoo has several educational programs for both adults and children to enable them understand more about wildlife. Here you will get to see the world's smallest monkeys, clap with seals, and see dolphins rotate in midair. There is also a petting zoo where you learn how to nurture animals. The main attraction in this zoo is the albino gorilla, which is one of its kind on earth.

16. Gaudi House Museum

There is no way you can visit Barcelona and see all the wonderful and beautiful works and not pay homage to the master who is non-other than Antoni Gaudí. The house is found inside the Park Güell in Barcelona. It is open to the public and contains furniture and objects that were designed by the architect.

The building was not designed by Gaudi but by Francesc Berenguer i Mestres and built by Casanovas i Pardo. Gaudi simply did the signing and it was built between 1903 and 1905. Gaudi was not the original owner. The house was put up for sale but no one bought it so Gaudi bought the house for himself and lived in it together with his father and niece. He lived there until some years before he committed himself to building the Sagrada Familia where he lived in the workshop.

This building has four floors whereby the first two floors are filled with a collection that is open to the public. The basement is closed to the public while the Enric Casanelles Library that is housed in the two upper floors is accessible with permission sought in advance.

Chapter 4: When To Visit Barcelona

Barcelona is great for visiting all year round. Actually, you will find it enjoyable even when you visit during the winter months of January and February. The city usually averages between 9-10 degrees C with sunny skies and pretty blue (clear) skies. This is usually considered comfortable weather. April-June and September to November also have similar temperatures.

August is the best visiting time if you don't mind crowds. At this time, you will notice that almost 10% of the shops will be closed between mid-august and early September given that owners usually go on vacation during this period. However, at the CBD, you will find lots of open shops and restaurants.

Note: Although Barcelona has many beaches, the locals might not really appreciate if you walk around with beachwear when going to church, or visiting restaurants.

Barcelona visitor information

You can check out the Visitor Information office on:

> http://www.barcelonaturisme.com/wv3/en/page/38/tourist-information-points.html

Or contact the office through +34 932 853 834 Monday-Saturday 08:00-20:00, Sundays and Holidays 08:00-14:00.

Chapter 5: Things To Do While In Barcelona

There are several activities that will enable you come alive and enjoy the true Barcelona experience.

According to the site TimeOutBarcelona, the following are some of the things you should do while in Barcelona.

- Discover the city on foot. The city is big but still is the perfect size for you to walk. Stroll around as you check out the city's gardens, parks, and buildings.

- Admire the old and the new. Thanks to Gaudi and modernistic buildings, Barcelona offers a wide range of building artistry as the two styles of architecture stand side by side in boldness.

- Attend a concert. Go listen to some good quality live music at the Razzmatazz and Apolo. Better yet, Barcelona is known to host international music festivals so do attend if there is one going on at the time of your visit. Some of the major festivals include Epiphany (5th/6th January), Carnival (February/March), Dia de Sant Jordi (23rd April), Formula One Spanish Grand Prix (May), Primavera Sound Festival (May/June), Grec Festival (Mid-June to early August).

- See where Picasso spent the days of his youth. Barcelona is not only the city of art but also a place that the great artists also dwelled. Follow in Picasso's footsteps walking down C/Reina Cristina and then crossing over to number 3 on C/Mercè to see where his family lived even though the building was destroyed.

- Enjoy fresh seafood. You cannot claim to have visited this Mediterranean city and not have sampled its seafood. The La Mar Salada and Can Solé display fresh seafood every day and this should whet your appetite to try some. You can also visit the Rias de Galicia for some fine and luxurious dining. You should expect to spend about €10 for a standard menu del dia.

- Get to know the history of the city by visiting its museums. Some of these include National Art Museum, Science Museum, Museu Historica de Catalunya, Museu De La Xocolata, Maritime Museum, CCCB (Barcelona Contemporary Cultural Center), Fundacio Joan Miro, Museu Picasso etc.

- Pick your food using toothpicks. Pick up the tapas, vermouths, and pintxos.

Pintxos

- Go to Raval and see what small businesses are doing. Raval has been assumed to be a place for prostitutes and drifters but actually you will see the other side of it that shows urban culture, music and good food.

- Climb mount Montjuïc. Give your legs a challenge to have a great view of the city and see the Olympic stadium and the telecommunications tower designed by Santiago.

- Go to the beaches: Barcelona has some of the finest beaches in Europe and has actually been named the #1 beach city in the world by National Geographic. Beach season often starts in mid March until mid November. The beaches are busiest between May and September. Some of the beaches include Llevant, Nova Mar Bella, Bogatell, Nova Icària, Somorrostro, Barceloneta, Sant Miquel, Sant Sebastià.

- Cruise several miles of beachfront boardwalk right from Barceloneta.

- Wander around Barri Gòtic in Ciutat Vella, the fairly intact pseudo medieval center of the city.

- Ensure to ride the Cable Way from the seafront to the Montjuïc mountain in Sants-Montjuïc

- Take coffee at Plaça dels Àngels in Ciutat Vella as you enjoy the whiteness of MACBA and enjoy the best street skate tricks in Barcelona.

- Watch a match at Camp Nou

- Sail on a classic yacht: http://www.classicsailbcn.eu/

Chapter 6: Food and Accommodation in Barcelona

Food

You should expect the following price ranges for a typical meal, inclusive of a soft drink:

Budget: Up to €10

Midrange: Between €10 and €25

Splurge: Over €25.

Accommodation

There are many accommodation options in Barcelona including cheap decent apartments, guesthouses, five star hotels, hostels etc. For specific accommodation information in the different districts, you can check here: Barceloneta, Sants-Montjuïc, Ciutat Vella (Gothic Quarter), Gràcia and Eixample. The links have details listings of accommodation.

You should expect to spend $35- $295 for a 3 star and below accommodation, $68-$552 for 4 star and $133-$612 for 5 star.

- *Look Barcelona Bruc Guest House, Eixample Dreta (Right)*

The doubles start from €119 inclusive of bed and breakfast. Contact CarrerBruc 96, +34 670 251225, Lookbarcelona.com.

- *Praktik Bakery, Eixample Dreta*

It has seventy-four rooms, which are not quite big but are still the right size. Doubles start from €60 room only. Contact

Carrer de Provença 279, +34 934 880061, hotelpraktikbakery.com

- *Retrome, Eixample Dreta*

It has eleven rooms and four apartments. It has Dutch and German furniture plus hand painted glass wall tiles. Doubles go from €80 room-only. Contact Carrer de Girona 85, +34 931 744037, retrome.net/Barcelona.

- *TOC, Eixample Esquerra (Left)*

This is actually a hostel. Dorm beds start from €12.75, en suite doubles from €63.50. Contact Gran Via de les CortsCatalanes 580, +34 934 534425.

- *Casa Bella Gracia, Gràcia*

This was once a carpentry workshop and it is located in Gràcia, away from the crowds. Doubles start from €65 room-only. Contact Carrer de SantAgustí 4, +34 638 493428, casabellagracia.com.

- *Tailor's, Sant Antoni*

This was once a tailor's workshop that was designed in the thirties. It is now a small charming hostel with basic old school dorms but the prices are fair. On the roof, there is a terrace for activities such as cycling, photography, and walking. Dorm beds start from €12. Contact Carrer de Sepúlveda 146, +34 932 505684.

- *H10 Port Vell, Harbourside*

This hotel has a great view of the harbor from the guest rooms. There is a roof terrace with a pool. Breakfast which will cost you an extra €19 or you can simply have some at the nearby Barceloneta market for a few Euros. Doubles start from €109 room-only. Contact Pas de SotaMuralla 9, +34 933 103065.

- *Chic&basic Port Barcelona Apartments, Raval*

These are ten apartments and each of them has a lounge, a sofa bed, a double bedroom, and a kitchen. They charge €59 a night. Contact Carrer de l'Est 21, +34 933 027111.

- *We Boutique Hotel, Arc de Triomf*

This hotel is situated inside a modernist apartment that is right next to Ciutadella park. It has many used retro furniture and has only six rooms. Doubles from €70 inclusive of bed and breakfast. Contact Ronda de Sant Pere 70, +34 932 503991, weboutiquehotel.com.

- *Yurbban Trafalgar, Born*

The hotel is a former textile factory and contains fifty-six rooms. On the roof, there are lounges and a plunge pool. Do not think too much about the weird signs like "Only for authorized personnel", this was once a factory. Doubles from €120 room-only. Contact Carrer de Trafalgar 30, +34 932 680727, yurbban.com.

- *Gran Hotel Torre Catalunya*

This is a four star hotel and is situated in the village of Sants-Montjuïc. It has stylish and modern furniture, satellite TV, an eclectic bar that serves great cocktails and they offer spa treatment. Price on multiple dates £83.88 per night, a single room.

- *BarceloSants*

It is easy to access since it is directly connected to the Barcelona International Airport and is near the train station. It costs $123 per night. Contacts Plaçadels Països Catalans, s/n, 08014 Barcelona, Spain. Phone:+34 935 03 53 00

- *Olivia Balmes Hotel*

It is a modern building that is opposite the Provenca Metro stop. The charges are $191 for a room. Contacts Carrer de Balmes, 117, 08008 Barcelona, Spain. Phone:+34 932 14 41 63

- *Casa Camper Hotel Barcelona*

It is located in Ciutat Vella. It located near the Centre de Cultura Contemporania de Barcelona, Casa Batllo and Palau de la Musica Catalana. Also nearby are Placa de Catalunya and Las Ramblas. They charge $311+ for a room. Contact Carrer Elisabets n.11, 08001 Barcelona, Catalonia, Spain +34 933 426 280. You can also check their site www.casacamper.com.

- *Mercer Hotel Barcelona*

The hotel is set in the old city. It is a 3-minute walk from the Jaume I metro station and 500m from the Museu Picasso (art museum). They charge from $331 for rooms. Contacts CarrerdelsLledó, 7, 08003 Barcelona, Spain. Phone:+34 933 10 74 80.

Conclusion

Once again thank you for choosing *Lost Travelers*!

I hope this book was able to provide you with the best travel tips when visiting Barcelona.

And we hope you enjoy your travels.

"Travel Brings Power And Love Back To Your Life"

- Rumi

Finally, if you enjoyed this book, then I'd like to ask you for a favor, would you be kind enough to leave a review for this book on Amazon? It'd be greatly appreciated!

➢ Simply search the keywords "Barcelona Lost Travelers" on Amazon or go to our Author page "Lost Travelers" to review.

Your satisfaction is important to us! If you were not happy with the book please email us with the title, your comment and suggestion so we may consider any improvements and serve you better in the next edition.

➢ Email: SevenTreeImprove@gmail.com

Thank you and good luck!

NOTES

NOTES

NOTES

NOTES

Preview Of 'Vienna: The Ultimate Vienna Travel Guide By A Traveler For A Traveler

What comes to mind when you hear the mention of Vienna? Is it the world's famous coffee houses, its famous heuriger or do you think of neighborhoods that are almost a millennia old? If you know a little bit about the city, you probably understand that it is the capital of Austria and the largest of the nine states of Austria housing nearly a third of Austria's entire population.

What you don't know is that it is the 6th largest city by population within the city limits in the EU and was once (in the early 20th century) the largest German-speaking city in the world before the split of Austro-Hungarian Empire during World War 1 when the city had about 2 million residents. It now hosts the 2nd largest number of German speakers after Berlin and is home to OPEC and UN. It has also been ranked as one of the most livable cities in the world several times according to the Quality of Life Survey, the most prosperous city in the world according to the UN-Habitat and one of the best in terms of culture of innovation and a lot more. Do you also know that it receives well over 3 million tourists every single year? Well, if the Baroque castles, gardens and the famous 19th century Ringstrasse lined with park, monuments, and grand buildings is anything to go by, I'd visit this wonderful city as often as possible.

Vienna, famously referred to as the city of music and the city of dreams, is undoubtedly one of those places you'd want to visit before you die. With a rich history going back to the 1st century AD, you can bet that it has seen a lot throughout its years of existence. This coupled with its strategic geographical location near Czech Republic, Slovakia and Hungary, it is certain that it plays an important role both as a political, economic and cultural center. Besides, its historic center has been designated a UNESCO World Heritage Site making it even more attractive to the world over.

If you are planning to visit Vienna, let this book be your guide to make your visit truly worthwhile. We will take a journey through the pages of history as we move to the present then narrow it down to the top places to visit, museums, art galleries and a lot more.

Check out the rest of Vienna: The Ultimate Vienna Travel Guide on Amazon by simply searching it.

Check Out Our Other Books

Below you'll find some of our other popular books that are on Amazon and Kindle as well. Simply search the titles below to check them out. Alternatively, you can visit our author page (Lost Travelers) on Amazon to see other work done by us.

- ➢ Vienna: The Ultimate Vienna Travel Guide By A Traveler For A Traveler

- ➢ Barcelona: The Ultimate Barcelona Travel Guide By A Traveler For A Traveler

- ➢ London: The Ultimate London Travel Guide By A Traveler For A Traveler

- ➢ Istanbul: The Ultimate Istanbul Travel Guide By A Traveler For A Traveler

- ➢ Vietnam: The Ultimate Vietnam Travel Guide By A Traveler For A Traveler

- ➢ Peru: The Ultimate Peru Travel Guide By A Traveler For A Traveler

- ➢ Australia: The Ultimate Australia Guide By A Traveler For A Traveler

- ➢ Japan: The Ultimate Japan Travel Guide By A Traveler For A Traveler

- New Zealand: The Ultimate New Zealand Travel Guide By A Traveler For A Traveler

- Dublin: The Ultimate Dublin Travel Guide By A Traveler For A Traveler

- Thailand: The Ultimate Thailand Travel Guide By A Traveler For A Traveler

- Iceland: The Ultimate Iceland Travel Guide By A Traveler For A Traveler

- Santorini: The Ultimate Santorini Travel Guide By A Traveler For A Traveler

- Italy: The Ultimate Italy Travel Guide By A Traveler For A Traveler

You can simply search for these titles on the Amazon website to find them.

CPSIA information can be obtained
at www.ICGtesting.com
Printed in the USA
LVOW13s2203190217
524731LV00016B/1325/P